My Mess, His Grace!

My Mess, His Grace!

*How God Swept me up
and Deep-Cleaned my chaos*

KRISTIE MCPHEETERS

My Mess, His Grace!

Copyright © 2023 by Kristie McPheeters. All rights reserved.

No part of this publication may be reproduced, stored in a retrieval system or transmitted in any way by any means, electronic, mechanical, photocopy, recording or otherwise without the prior permission of the author except as provided by USA copyright law.

ISBN: 979-8-88759-432-3 (paperback)
ISBN: 979-8-88759-433-0 (ebook)
ISBN: 979-8-88759-480-4 (hardcover)

Dedication

I would like to dedicate this book
to the following people:

My Children

They are now amazing adults who have been by my side and have been my biggest cheerleaders. Nathan, Nadeen, Ben, and Angelica have all been with me through the trenches of life. Thank you for your genuine heart and love. Thank you for all your support. I am so thankful God chose me to be your mom.

My Grandparents

You have always shown me who Jesus is and how much He loves me. Your unwavering commitment to Jesus helped mold me into who I am today. I am forever grateful to you, Grandma Peggy, Grandma Themis, and Grandpa Bill for introducing me to our Lord and Savior.

My Tribe

Donna, Marcy, Deeny, Dettie, Teresa, Michelle, Lorraine, Richelle, Gina and Jessica thank you for speaking truth into my life and being there every step of the way through this crazy roller coaster of life. You are forever my best friends! You are the best friends a lady could ask for; we call each other family.

My Mom

Thank you, Mom, for allowing me to share our stories. But more importantly, thank you for cleaning up your life and following Jesus. You have a heart of gold. I love you!

My Mother-in-Law

Thank you for being the best mother-in-law a girl could ask for. I pray that you are looking down from heaven and feeling blessed by the impact you made on my life. Not a day goes by that I don't miss you. I love you to heaven and back.

All Young Women with a Heavy Heart

Life has beaten you up, and you need up for air. You need some joy in your life and to recognize God's grace. Jesus loves you, and so do I. I pray that this book blesses you and speaks to you where needed. I pray that God shows you that He always holds you in the palm of His hands.

Preface

Around 2004, the Lord prompted me to write this book. When you have been through trials and challenges in life, it cannot be in vain. There has to be a lesson learned and something to teach and share with others. When I was sitting with my family at our monthly Family Fellowship gathering, I decided to share with the ladies how I felt led to write. They were all so encouraging and would ask me from time to time if I had started the book. I avoided writing the book because it required me to be vulnerable and put all my business out for the world to see. I'm not proud of the choices I've made over the years, but I hope that you will learn from my mistakes. This book isn't to glorify the bad choices I've made by any means. It is meant to encourage you to seek God and embrace His amazing grace on your journey in this life.

God has graciously invited us into His mysterious story, and we are being watched by a cloud of witnesses to see how we play this out. Did you know that we have more information about God than people like Moses, Issac, Jacob, and David from the Bible did? They had little knowledge compared to what we have been blessed with, yet they still obeyed God. Our role on this Earth is so important. What we say no to now will affect us twenty years from now. I hope that by being obedient to the Lord in finally writing this book, like He had asked me to do so many years ago, that you will be blessed twenty or more years down the road.

I pray that you embrace God's love and grace for your life. He loves you more than you know.

About The Author

Kristie McPheeters is a born and raised Southern Californian momma of four, with two grandsons and a heart to help young ladies navigate through life's many trials. She loves Jesus, camping, hiking, adventures with her amazing man, and family time. She loves her nieces and nephews with all her heart and has the desire to serve them where she can.

Chapter 1

Choices

Hey, girl! How's it going? I have so much I want to share with you, but I don't want to vomit my life all over you through this book. I hope to show you how much you are loved, not forgotten.

My story

One Wednesday night I was at a mid-week service, and during worship, this girl named Rina, whom I didn't know at the time, tapped me on the shoulder and said, "God wants you to know that He hasn't forgotten you." She has no idea how profound her words were. Those words were straight from God's lips to her heart to my heart. You see, I was a newly single mom of three and life had just gotten real hard once more.

I was no stranger to hard. It started in my childhood. My mom had three children when she was just a teenager. She had my brother Ricky when she was fifteen, me when she was sixteen, and my brother Eric right before her seventeenth birthday. She wasn't ready to be a mom, she wasn't even finished being a kid. My mom had been very hurt and wounded as a young girl, and she made some poor choices that led her to a rough life of drug abuse. That phrase "hurting people hurt people" took life in her heart, as she became physically, mentally, and emotionally abusive to my older brother and me. I'm not leaving my younger brother out. He was adopted out at birth, which of course added more hurt to my mom's already broken heart.

Needless to say, addiction controlled a large part of my life. Although I wasn't addicted to anything, my mom sure was. Her drug of choice was methamphetamines, which are a stimulant. I'm not a doctor or scientist, so I'm going to give the streetwise verbiage. I remember at the age of four hearing words like whites, reds, uppers, downers, Quaaludes, and weed. I didn't know what they were but had to witness them while growing up. I later learned that whites, uppers, coke, speed, and meth were all stimulants. Reds, downers, Quaaludes, and weed were all to relax you and get you high.

Random people came in and out of our home and lives. I wasn't sure if they would come over to buy from my mom, or if they were just her "druggy friends." That's what I called them. I know that sounds mean, but these random strangers would come over, and then all hell would break loose. My mom would go through her vicious cycle of being happy, to sad, to mad, to rage, then to blaming everyone for her roller-coaster behavior.

MY MESS, HIS GRACE!

That is one thing about an addict: they never take ownership of their behavior. They take the victim mentality. Everything they do is because of how you made them feel, or what you did or didn't do. My mom was no different. Her perception of reality was altered because of the drugs.

Don't get me wrong, my mom would go through her loving stages. Every time she hit what we thought was rock bottom, she would go to rehabilitation and get clean and stay clean for a good while. It was hard to wrap my head around how she could be clean for one or more years, then fall off the bandwagon, causing the vicious cycle to start all over again. When my mom was clean, she was amazing—very loving and everything you would want in a mom.

It confused me, as she would be one way then the other. I never knew what I was coming home to. I remember one time I came home from the beach with my friend Gina and found my mom lying on the couch with her leg elevated. As soon as she saw me, she said, "This is your fault, you little B." Well, it obviously wasn't my fault because I had just walked in after being gone all day. I found out she had pulled her shenanigans on my brother, and he wasn't having it. They wrestled by the refrigerator, and she sprained her foot. Thank the Lord she couldn't get up off the couch to lay into me like she normally would. It seemed like every time she was mad, it was my fault.

In first grade, it was my responsibility to have the house cleaned before she got home from work. I had to clean the dishes, vacuum, make my bed, clean my room, and tidy up the bathroom. I apparently didn't clean the dishes in hot enough water and didn't get all the food off of the plate. That was enough to send her out in a rage, yelling, screaming, and kicking me. Nothing I did was ever up to her standards.

Because of this, I was fearful of her for a good portion of my life. I was a latchkey child from kindergarten to the fourth grade. I would get out of school and walk home to be left at home alone. I lived in Inglewood, California, at the time. If you know Inglewood, you know how bad the area was at that time. While growing up there, I was followed home, jumped by two girls, and our house had been broken into. So not only did I not have a safe home to go to, but I was also afraid most of the time.

My stepdad would have his occasional drinks, but drugs were not his thing. My dad really loved my mom and us kids, so he stuck it out for twenty-two years before he couldn't take it anymore. I don't believe their divorce was even finalized before they both moved on and shortly remarried. Thankfully I was out of the house when this all happened.

Yet, I was so blessed to come from a large, God-loving family. I know this sounds so strange based on what I just shared of my mom's story. But it is true. God held my hand through everything in my life.

The choice to see good and forgive

Looking back, I can see His hand. Before I started the fifth grade, my grandma decided it would be better for us to live at her home in Lawndale, and she would move into one of our duplex houses in Inglewood. My brother's godmother Toby lived in the front house. Lawndale was a huge step up from Inglewood at the time. I was never followed home or jumped again. But I still had my mom to go home to. Within a month of the move, Toby was followed home, raped, and murdered in the house we had just moved out of, the house my grandma was now living in. My grandma and stepdad both decided to sell the Inglewood houses and add on to the Lawndale home so we could all live together.

My grandma moving in with us and doing life together was God-ordained. Now I had someone who would intervene when things got rough. I had someone praying for me and looking out for my best interest. I didn't have to live in fear of my mom the same way anymore, and I didn't have to worry about walking back and forth to school unless I wanted to walk with my friends.

So, while my mom still did drugs and found new druggy friends, I no longer felt alone. I now had a family at home, not just a house to go home too.

So, despite my rough upbringing, I chose to see the good. God continued to hold my hand through many of life's trials, whether through a friend, family member, coworker, or random stranger. God has shown me over and over where He was during every trial. Have you ever gone through something and came out on the other side thinking, *WOW! That was so God.* The worship song "You Never Let Go" by Matt Redman has been such a pillar in my life. It resonates with my spirit.

If you had a rough upbringing, it is so easy to fall into the victim mentality. But let me tell you, you have a choice. You have a choice to live in unforgiveness or to forgive and have freedom. You're probably thinking, *Kristie, you have no idea what I've been through.* You're right! I don't! But I can guarantee you that I've been through my fair share, and I've had to decide every single time to forgive or hold on. I'm not saying forgiveness is easy, but I will say it is worth it. The freedom that comes from releasing that hurt, person, or moment in time is beyond what you can imagine.

Forgiveness is a tricky thing. Most people have the wrong idea of what forgiveness is.

Forgiveness is not:

- Having to hang out with that person who hurt you
- Feeling warm and fuzzy about that person who hurt you
- Going back to the abusive relationship even though they said sorry
- Giving your time
- Replying to a text, phone call, or any other form of communication
- Putting yourself in a compromised position

- Creating an unhealthy boundary
- Holding a grudge

Forgiveness is:

- A choice
- A command by God
- The way to love unconditionally

Forgiveness equals:

- Freedom
- Growth
- Hope
- Future
- A gift
- Your best interest
- Peace of mind
- Healing for your soul

Matthew 18:21–22 says, "Then Peter came to Him and said, 'Lord how often shall my brother sin against me, and I forgive him? Up to seven times?' Jesus said to him, 'I do not say to you, up to seven times, but up to seventy times seven.'"

I don't believe Jesus is saying forgive four hundred and ninety times, but he is saying to forgive as many times as it takes. I'm not saying this is easy. But it is worth it. When we forgive, we are being set free, and there is nothing like walking in freedom.

About twenty years ago, I heard something that resonated with me, not sure where I heard it: "Every time the scenario or person pops up in your head, say out loud, I choose to forgive [insert name] and release them to God." Let me tell you there were times when I had to choose to forgive someone a hundred times in the day. I'm not even joking. It is real. But I decided I wasn't going to become a bitter old lady like some of the elderly ladies on the street that I grew up on. They would get downright a little crazy, popping their little faces out the window to yell at the kids playing outside. Those cute, little old ladies just got ugly. For real, I didn't want to be like that, so I made the decision not to be.

Now not all the older ladies on our street were bitter. We had Aunt Bunny, who lived across the street, and she was the sweetest. She wasn't really my aunt, but that's what we called her. I believe God put me in her heart a lot. I didn't realize it then, but all these years later, I see how God used her to show me He was there with me all along. Aunt Bunny would invite me over all the time to do creative things, like quilting, crocheting, arts and crafts, and to go to church. I told her I wanted to make a quilt for my parents for their anniversary, and she went and bought all the stuff to help me make it. I cut all the little squares so perfectly, with her help, of course. She was so patient with me. But I must have been running out of time because she came over to our house on my parents' anniversary with the quilt wrapped and gave it to me to give to them. That was the sweetest thing. Now that I'm crocheting blankets as an adult, I know how much money and time it takes. God used Aunt Bunny to show me how much He loves me and that He saw me and what I needed.

But since I was surrounded by several grabby old ladies, I could have chosen to dislike them and not trust Aunt Bunny. But I chose to like them and think they are the cutest things. Those little old ladies in my neighborhood experienced so much in life that made them who they are today. And, yes, some of them chose to be bitter. Aunt Bunny chose to be happy. All of them went through more than we could imagine.

You see, it is all about choices. My choice to be bitter at my abusive childhood or to see the good in my extended family. My choice to forgive or to remain angry at those who had hurt me. And those ladies had a choice to be bitter in their old age or remain happy and pleasant.

Our lives are full of choices. We must choose to forgive to live a happy, healthy life. We must choose better for ourselves regularly.

Choosing boundaries from the Lord

We also have the choice to create boundaries for ourselves. After I left home, it had gotten really bad. My mom and her druggy friends decided it would be a great idea to become trash diggers! They wanted to make arts and crafts with all the "goodies" they would find. They would make arts and crafts to sell to buy drugs. Now I shouldn't knock this because they weren't stealing or taking from people, they were trying to be upright druggies. Seriously! I'm laughing as I'm writing this because it is so out there. In Lawndale, everyone knew each other. So, I had friends reaching out to me to let me know they saw my mom trash digging. I was mortified.

I decided I would go over there to see what was going on and take my niece, whom my mom was watching at the time, lunch from Carl's Jr. All I can say is my niece was very happy to see me and my mom was not. My mom had turned our living room into a mini–Hobby Lobby from the trash bins. I'm not even kidding. The entire living room was filled. It had containers full of arts and crafts she got from TG&Y, and it was organized. She would be up all night, taking meth, to organize her arts and crafts, aka trash. What in the world was happening? I thought I had seen it all up until this point. Needless to say, my mom didn't watch my niece after that. My brother and sister-in-law decided to put her in preschool.

With my childhood and all that I saw from my mother after I left the house, I developed post-traumatic stress disorder. I learned I couldn't trust anyone, especially my mom. The problem was I knew God but didn't know how to fully give my mom or any of them that hurt me to God at this time. I just knew I needed protection, so I was going to protect myself. To do this, I put up boundaries. I subconsciously knew that I needed boundaries. This is before the book *Boundaries* by Dr. Henry Cloud and John Townsend was even published.

MY MESS, HIS GRACE!

Right then and there, I decided if my mom was on her druggy binge, I would not be around her. If she was clean, then I would. In my head and heart, I had to do this to protect myself. Please don't start putting up walls between you and people. I now see in hindsight that I should have looked at my relationship with my mom through the eyes of Christ, not through my eyes. Boundaries are amazing, but you have to make sure the boundaries you are putting up are from the Lord and not from your place of hurt or fear. If you put up boundaries that are not from the Lord, you will wind up hurting people.

Girl, you have a choice. Whatever it is you are holding on to, I want to encourage you to *choose* to forgive and let go so you will have a happier, more fulfilled life. Choose to see the good in life and choose God-oriented boundaries to protect yourself.

Is there something or someone you need to choose to forgive or let go of? I would like to encourage you to write in the journal portion of this chapter and list out everyone and everything you are choosing to forgive and give to God—even if you have to do it hundreds of times a day. Trust me, it will get easier!

Is there an experience you only see as negative? Journal everything that could be seen as a positive that came from or happened during that experience.

Journal Notes

Journal Notes

Chapter 2

The Unforeseen

The saying that everything in life is a choice probably sounds blah, but let me tell you, I have made good choices and some very poor choices along the way. And with each choice comes consequences! They can be good, bad, or just what it is. However, I would prefer the good consequences.

My story

When I was engaged and getting married in three weeks, I was sitting at church during worship and filled with the Holy Spirit, just really in the zone, and I heard the Lord say to me, "You are not to marry him. He is not your husband!" I said, "What? Oh no, Lord, I'm marrying him. The invitations are out, and my mom has paid for everything. My bridesmaids all had their dresses and family had bought tickets to fly to California from Oregon and Washington." I reacted in full-blown

MY MESS, HIS GRACE!

disobedience and rebellion. I didn't think about it or pray about it. I just said I'm marrying him.

Let's just say I learned the hard way that I would reap what I sowed and there would be consequences. After eight years of marriage, my husband decided he had fallen in love with my friend and wanted a divorce. When the affair first started, I had an inkling that something was going on. I became keenly aware of both of their actions. She was my friend and my neighbor. We coached soccer together and our husbands coached baseball together. We would have barbecues with each other and watch the games and MMA fights at each other's houses. I would say we all got close, which made the betrayal all the worse.

And here we were with a home and three children, and he wanted to leave. My poor choice delivered a slew of decisions for me to make. It was like sink or swim. Sell the house? Don't sell the house? Move to Arizona to be with his family? Move an hour away to be with my family? Leave everything behind or take everything I owned? Keep my wedding rings or sell them? Go to counseling? Don't go to counseling? The list went on and on. With so much uncertainty in my heart and mind, I didn't know if I was coming or going.

Well, I decided to have a yard sale and give *everything* away. I didn't care to keep anything. Looking back that wasn't a good idea to give it away for free because I needed money to feed and take care of my kids, but I just wanted to get the heck out of there and start fresh. This man pulled up in his truck and said he would give me a certain amount of money for everything because he could take it to Mexico and give everything to families in need. Well, that's all he had to say, and I gave it to him for free. I just wanted it all gone. At least the Lord used my poor financial choice for His good.

Since I didn't have any money for the kids and me to get us by until we got the money from the house sale, I decided to go to the pawn shop on our way out of town to pawn my two wedding ring sets to get us by. Then we moved an hour away to be with my side of the family. When my ex found out what I had done with the rings, he about lost his head. He said, "What did you do that for? You could have sold them for so much more on Craigslist." Okay, I know what you're thinking. How dumb could I be? Now I had made two very poor financial decisions. I never thought about Craigslist as an option. I just knew I didn't want the rings, and I needed the money.

From this, I learned that I had to be very careful not to make decisions when my heart and mind weren't grounded. I hope you never experience or have to experience infidelity. But I will tell you, it takes a while to get your heart and mind right when going through something like this. You're almost not in your body. Just strange feelings all around. I decided after this that counseling was probably a very good idea. Heck, the best one I've made so far.

I was really worried my kids were not going to be okay going through the divorce and being in split homes, going back and forth with mom and dad, changing schools, moving to another area, and starting at a new church. But we had to make a new normal. So, I made an appointment, and Praise God! Literally Praise God! The counselor watched the kids play and interact and talked with me, and she said, "Your kids are good." Then she said the most profound thing that really helped me through this time. She said, "If you're okay, your kids are going to be okay." I held on to her words like they were gold. And you know what? She was right.

Don't get me wrong: they were still kids and we were still going through a huge life change, but they were troopers. God showed me that He really does hold us during trying times, even if we don't feel Him.

I wish I could remember where I read this: "Keep your dignity when you leave that place or town." The night before we moved away, I read that, and it was confirmation to me that God didn't want me there, and He definitely wanted me to choose to keep my dignity. So, I chose to do so and hold my head high. I knew God had my back. This gave me strength I didn't know I needed.

Consequences for our choices

How we react and choose to handle the situation is up to us. But then our choices have consequences.

During this trial, I had made some good choices and some bad ones. Initially, I did not forgive my ex. But the consequence of that was the hate and bitterness that settled into my heart. It took me a good three years to really forgive. One day I just felt in my spirit that it was time to let this go. I called my ex-husband on his birthday and told him, "I am choosing to forgive you. I am not going to be mad anymore, and I'm not going to bring things up anymore." And just like that, I had no ill feelings. God loved me that day. He removed all the bitterness, rage, hurt, and anger. I was free! All because I chose to forgive him. I thought I was being nice by giving him forgiveness as a birthday gift, but God was really being nice to me and setting me free.

Galatians 5:1 says, "Stand fast therefore in the liberty by which Christ has made us free, and do not be entangled again with a yoke of bondage."

You would think being a Christian and having a relationship with God means that you can't fall into bondage. Well, I'm a living example that, yes, you can. If you feel a nudge in your spirit right now and God is telling you to walk away from a relationship, job, friendship, or any situation, I am pleading with you to please obey. Let me tell you, my friend, God is not a man that He should lie. He is a man of His word. If he is directing you, it is the truth. Don't go against the voice of God. That direction will lead you straight to bondage, a consequence of a poor choice.

I had to learn this the hard way. Have you ever heard or felt God leading you in a certain direction, but you ignored him? Have you ever felt uneasy in your spirit about the thing you were about to do? Like it just didn't feel right? I believe we have all been there.

MY MESS, HIS GRACE!

Probably not as dramatic as when I married someone He told me wasn't my husband, but you get the idea.

Oxford Languages' definition of bondage is "the state of being a slave."

The hard thing about bondage is it is really hard to get out of. While my ex-husband was having a two-and-a-half-year affair, I was in bondage. I couldn't have imagined my life any differently. We were both miserable. Although we had a home and children and loved each other because we had known each other since junior high, this affair changed me. I was consumed by the entire situation. I would look at his phone, follow him, and show up at places he thought he was safe to hide, calling and texting non-stop. That is insane. No one should ever live a life of fear and insecurity.

Satan's role

Even when God tells us not to do something, or we lean on the Lord to help us make our choices, we can make mistakes. We can make the wrong choice. Satan is very crafty. He gets you to fall for the wrong person or land the wrong job or any other situation, then tortures you after he gets you good and stuck in bondage.

Now I'm not going to glorify Satan. I just want to say the war we have within us is a spiritual battle, and we need to be aware of the fact that just like God is real, so is the enemy. The Bible tells us in Philippians 2:12, "Therefore, my beloved, as you have always obeyed, not as sin in my presence only, but now much more in my absence, work out your own salvation with fear and trembling." We have to make a conscious effort to use discernment. I am serious about the conscious effort part. The enemy is crafty, and if we aren't paying attention, we can get sucked into a situation we shouldn't be in.

1st Peter 5:8–11 tells us, "Be sober, be vigilant; because your adversary the devil walks about like a roaring lion, seeking whom he may devour. Resist him, steadfast in the faith, knowing that the same sufferings are experienced by your brotherhood in the world. But may the God of all grace, who called us to His eternal glory by Christ Jesus, after you have suffered a while, perfect, establish, strengthen and settle you."

I love God! Look how much He loves us. He warns us to be alert. We are human, and we all make mistakes and make the wrong choices. This morning I saw this meme on Facebook: "We all have pasts. We all made choices that maybe weren't the best ones. None of us are completely innocent, but we all get a fresh start every day to be a better person than we were yesterday." I love this. God's grace is sufficient for us, and his mercies are new every morning.

God can rescue you

Even when we make the wrong choice, despite the Lord's warnings, God will still show up to rescue us from our own self-made bondage.

When our spouse has an affair, we experience many emotional side effects.

During the affair, obsessive thoughts became my reality. I didn't yet have proof, so I would just obsess over details. My mind made up all kinds of crazy ideas to help me downplay what was happening before my eyes because I didn't want to be a crazy, jealous wife. He would pull out of our driveway, and a minute later she was pulling out of her driveway. He would come home, and a minute later she would pull into her driveway. This went on for years, and I couldn't help but think, "There they go again." She would know things about me that I had only shared with him and vice versa. When I would confront either of them, their reaction was the same. They would tell me, "You are crazy! This is all in your head."

I turned into someone I didn't recognize. I was losing weight, hair, and confidence and breaking out. Worse, I started blaming myself for everything. This situation made me think I was crazy. I would go to church, then turn around and fall right back into overthinking. The stress caused me to break out in what I thought was a rash, only later to find out I had shingles, which are brought on by stress. I couldn't sleep because my heart would race, and I would physically make myself sick to my stomach. When I went to the doctor for the rash, the doctor asked me what was going on, and I proceeded to give her a long list of all my ailments. She was on top of her game, and said, "Tell me everything that is going on with you and take as long as you need. Don't leave anything out." I told her everything from beginning to end in detail. The doctor told me, "First of all, you are not crazy. Your husband is having an affair." She gave me prescriptions for the upset tummy and the shingles and Xanax for the anxiety. I went home and told my husband that she gave me the Xanax, and he was upset, saying I didn't need that. But why would he say that since he was the one who kept telling me I was crazy?

I'm not an advocate for antidepressants. But I did take them for two of the three months. They did help me to keep a level head on the big day. On the big day, he was late coming home from work, and when I called him, I heard a little voice, "check his voicemail." Now that was crazy and not normal Kristie thinking. I guessed his password, and I was right. This had to be God. Because I never would have thought to check his voicemail before this. Lo and behold, she had left him a voicemail that said, "Hi, Baby. I miss you and want to see you this morning. I love you." That's when my body went hot and weak. I've never had anxiety before, so it was a very different feeling than I've ever experienced. I couldn't stand, and I literally fell to the ground in slow motion. I had no words and just felt overwhelmed. Not only was my heart broken, but I couldn't move my body for some time.

When I could move, I picked myself up off the floor, called his work, and had him paged. With my heart pounding, I said, "You cannot lie to me anymore. I just called your voicemail and heard her message. She wants to meet you this morning and she misses and loves you. You need to let her know that she needs to

My Mess, His Grace!

tell her husband today, or I will tell him." That poor guy had thought he was going crazy too. Long story short, she called her husband all right. But she told him that my husband was stalking her and that I was making up stories to hurt her.

I had gotten myself into this situation. I had chosen to marry him despite the warning from God. But God still showed up and rescued me. He was so on top of this day. My dad showed up out of nowhere, when he should have been at work, to see me, and then my cousin, who lived an hour away but had an interview close by that day, showed up a few minutes later with Starbucks in hand. Neither of them knew what had just happened at my house minutes before they got there. But God knew! He orchestrated their morning. Their showing up when they did was what I needed at that time.

My husband was a police officer, so the problem with the stalking allegations was *huge*. Her husband reported the stalking allegations to my husband's department. Before I got a heads-up about these allegations, Internal Affairs showed up at my house. Did I mention I was running a daycare at the time? My husband wanted me to run a daycare like my cousins because he saw how well they were doing. Needless to say, the timing of Internal Affairs showing up at my house was not ideal. I had my youngest son who just turned three years old at home with the daycare children. The officers were asking if I knew that my husband was stalking this lady who lived four doors down to the left of us. Without hesitation, I said, "He is not stalking her. Those two are having an affair." They left, and when I looked out the window, I saw them putting her in the police car. No . . . she didn't get arrested. They just needed to talk to her in private. Thankfully, she came clean with the officers.

The journey to moving on starts now. Now that everything's out in the open. It's time to handle business.

Can you remember an unforeseen time in your life? Can you see where God intervened? Journal below how God showed up.

Journal Notes

Journal Notes

Chapter 3

A Broken Picker

We joke in our family that we have a broken picker. For some reason, some of us only picked the wrong guys to allow into our lives. My friend, I could tell you so many stories. For some reason, I would attract the wrong guys over and over. Later I learned, I had emotionally unhealthy boundaries. It took me fifty years to get it right. I've dated physically and emotionally abusive men, cheaters, drunkards, liars, manipulators, and downright dishonest men. I didn't seem to know my worth.

Let's be honest. We know a red flag when we see it. But why is it that we ignore the red flags? Are we so full of ourselves that we think we can fix that person or that we can change them? Chances are, that won't happen. People usually are who they show they are. Now I'm not saying *everyone*. God can definitely do miracles. But don't get stuck in bondage with someone in hopes that you can fix them or that they will change for you.

Red flags indicate exactly that: a warning to run! I can say this because I didn't run. That's why I wound up in very hurtful relationships, hoping for a better turnout. I hope you won't make the same mistakes I have.

You are a daughter of the most-high King! A royal priesthood. You deserve nothing but God's best. I would hear this over and over through the years, but my heart didn't grasp it. I knew the words, but I had only experienced being treated *less* than God's best, which made me think that's all that was out there for me.

With every relationship I was in, I was left grasping for nibbles of the dangling carrot. If that person would spend the bare minimum of time with me, I would take it. If that person would put their friends first, I wouldn't complain. I was in very empty relationships with men that didn't give me the time of day. With my ex-husband, it was great until it wasn't. I spent most of our marriage trying to get nibbles from the dangling carrot.

When I got divorced, I dated off and on. However, these men were either emotionally abusive or just not emotionally available. Yet, I believed the lie that this was all I deserved. What a very lonely place to be. But because I knew nothing else, I didn't even realize I was lonely.

Ladies, I want you to know that you should never settle. If you see red flags, you should reconsider the relationship you're in. Never just take what you can get.

When you date someone, make sure they don't display any of these non-negotiable behaviors or problems:

My Mess, His Grace!

- Lying
- Cheating
- Emotionally unavailable
- Physically unavailable
- Addicted to drugs
- Alcoholism
- Gambling
- Controlling/manipulative or devious
- Not trustworthy
- Disrespectful
- Poor communication/unable to resolve conflict
- Bullying
- Drama
- Fearful or low self-esteem
- Financially dishonest
- Gaslighting
- Hostile or full of anger issues
- Negative and overly critical
- Unhappy
- Narcissistic
- Codependent
- Excessively jealous
- Exploiter (user)
- Selfish—self-absorbed, self-centered, self-loving, pompous, or self-gratifying
- Vain
- Unpredictable

These red flags apply to friendships as well. Proverbs 4:23 tells us, "Keep your heart with all diligence, for out of it spring the issues of life." If you settle in the areas listed above, you will not have the fulfilling relationship you are looking for.

If you have a broken picker, like I did, please pray and ask God to show you through His eyes what he wants for you.

Before my divorce was final, I remember talking to my friend Robert and telling him that I didn't know what I would do if I met someone who actually wanted to spend time with me. How sad is that?

I am so happy to say that I am in a very happy, healthy relationship for the first time in my life. Our relationship is free of the behaviors and problems listed above. Praise God! He treats me with love, and guess what? He likes spending time with me. We've been dating for the past three years and he hasn't changed. He is the same as he was from the very beginning when we became friends four years ago.

I won't say it was always easy. Because of my past relationships, I had to work through a lot of my own insecurities and fears. But he has been so patient with me as the Lord healed my broken heart.

Over the past twenty years, I've learned through trial and error. I would like to help you not make the same mistakes I did. If you are in a relationship or friendship that just isn't settling well with you, please take a moment to write down the pros and cons of being in this relationship in the journal section. Pray over the list and ask God to show you His will for your life and whether you should continue in the relationship or walk

My Mess, His Grace!

away. Just to be clear, I'm not an advocate for divorce, but sometimes it is necessary.

If you have been hurt in this relationship or friendship, please take the time to allow God to heal your heart. The worst thing you can do is jump into another relationship right away. I've seen so many people relationship-hop over the years, and it makes my heart so sad. It is okay to go years without dating.

God loves you so much, and He wants to heal your heart of any and all hurts. Psalms 34:18 says, "The Lord is near to those who have a broken heart; And saves such as have a contrite spirit."

Do you have a broken picker? Ask the Lord to show you your relationships through His eyes. I would like to challenge you to ask the Lord to open the doors He wants opened and to close the doors He wants closed. Believe me when I tell you, the doors He wants shut will slam shut fast. Ask God to reveal His will to you in your relationships. Journal below what God puts on your heart. Pray on it, meditate on it, and then obey His words to you.

Journal Notes

Journal Notes

Chapter 4

Starting Over

Have you ever had to start all over in life? It is challenging and emotional. Right before my sixteenth birthday, I knew I had to make a drastic change in my life because I was making all the wrong decisions.

My story

When I was twelve years old, I had my first beer, which opened the door for the next four years.

Drinking became my coping mechanism, to avoid dealing with life. It became an every-weekend thing, then I started drinking during the week. Where in the world does a twelve-year-old buy beer? I honestly don't remember. We would go to a friend's house every Friday and Saturday, where bands would play, and we would drink.

My brother was always in a band, and all the cute band guys would come over and practice in our garage.

My parents were really cool about our house being the neighborhood hangout. I think my dad allowed it because then he had his eye on us. My mom had different reasons. She wanted to party too. She would be right there in the mix, chatting with the girls and getting high with whoever wanted to get high with her. This was so hard for me. I didn't want her partying with my friends. But since she had started doing drugs at such a young age, her mind stayed at that young age. So she always thought she was younger than she really was.

This would get so awkward. I couldn't trust my mom's temperament, and now I couldn't trust her with my friends. She was very unpredictable. One time I really didn't feel well, so I went into her room to lay on her waterbed. It was always so warm and cozy. I thought for sure I could feel better if I just lay on her bed for an hour. But when I walked into her room, the room was full of smoke and my mom and two of my friends were getting high. I remember feeling like I had nowhere to go, and I was sick and stuck in this craziness.

This scenario would play out every day. It just never stopped. Eventually, I felt that if I couldn't beat them, then I should join them and find out what the hype was. So, I gave in and got high with them, and trust me when I tell you, smoking pot was definitely not for me. I blacked out, got nauseous, and just felt plain horrible. I couldn't understand what all the hype was about. Who in the world wants to feel out of control and physically sick? No thank you! Not me.

From there, my mom and friends started taking speed and cocaine. I thought they all had lost their darn mind. Until repeat: I gave in and started trying speed and cocaine with them. Speed was horrible and that was short-lived for me. Again, no thank you! Cocaine was very expensive and coming down from the drug was a horrible feeling. Going two to three days with no sleep makes you feel really wacky. Really what did my friends and mom get out of this type of partying? I was perfectly happy getting drunk. I didn't need all the other stuff. Of course, I didn't need to get drunk either, but at that time, I felt like I did.

God is and was so gracious to me. He pulled me out of that rut in my junior year of high school. One night I went to sleep in my grandma's room because I was afraid that my abusive boyfriend would try to sneak back into my room again. But it turned out I also needed to hide from my mom. At 3:00 a.m., she decided the dishes needed to be done, even though I had done them after school. But you can't speak rationally to someone who is under the influence. My mom stormed into my grandma's room to look for me. She was yelling and screaming all kinds of profanity, telling me I needed to get out of bed and wash the dishes right now. Was she serious? I had to get up for school in a few hours. All I can say is thank the Lord for my grandma. She spoke up and said, "She is not getting up to wash the dishes. She is going to sleep because she has school, and if you want the dishes done at three in the morning, you can wash them yourself."

The next morning, I was done. Put a fork in me. I was cooked, done, finished, and all the other terms for *over it*! I was tired and had no more fight in me. Between my abusive boyfriend and mom, I was losing all my joy. I didn't feel worthy of happiness. Why would I? All I knew was, I needed to get out of that house. I wasn't going to make it if I stayed there. The abuse was too much. The layers of hurt had been piled too high. I didn't talk to my boyfriend or my mom about it. But that day I had a plan. When I got to work that night, I called my aunt and uncle and asked if I could go live with them.

That night when I got home, I talked to my dad. I felt bad because I sort of lied. I told him if I stayed there, I wasn't going to graduate from high school. That wasn't entirely true. I had more than enough credits. However, if I stayed, I'm not sure where I would have wound up. But that was the only way he was going to let me go because he wanted me to graduate. The next morning my uncle picked me up from my house. When he got there, my mom was yelling and screaming from the streets about how much she hated me. You really can't talk rationally to someone when they are under the influence. Her words hurt me really bad, but I had to stay strong.

When I got to my aunt and uncle's house, I went through the motions, learning a new normal, and getting a fresh start. My aunt took me to enroll in the continuing education school where one of my cousins attended because I wanted to be with someone I knew.

The secretary at the school looked at me like I was crazy. She said, "You don't need to be here. You have more than enough credits to go across the street to the regular high school." I didn't care what people thought about the school I went to. I wanted to be where I felt I would be more comfortable. So my aunt enrolled me, and looking back, I know this was God-approved.

I met some Christian friends at school that I really connected with, and they helped me through the rest of school without alcohol and drugs. These friends Lisa and Laura invited me to church, Bible study, and to their house to hang out. We all became very close. Later on, Laura asked me to be her daughter's godmother, and Lisa asked me to be her maid of honor.

A do-over

In this new life I had created, I was high on God. Have you ever been high on God? Let me tell you that is the best high you can have. I've had both, and I would pick being filled with the Holy Spirit over getting high any day.

I am being very raw because I want you to know there is a way out. If you are struggling and trying to see where you fit in, just know that God always gives you a way out. He is standing next to you with open arms, waiting for you and wanting you to come to Him. Do you need a fresh start? A new beginning? God has a plan. His plan is to set you free. Take a few minutes to journal what you need to walk toward Him and away from your current life, and ask God how He would like to give you a fresh start. A clean slate. A new beginning.

Journal Notes

Journal Notes

Chapter 5

Forgiveness

We spoke a little bit about forgiveness already, but this topic is extremely important because forgiveness is one key to living a life of joy and freedom. I don't know about you, but I do not ever want a wedge between God and myself. Matthew 6:14–15 says, "For if you forgive men their trespasses, your Heavenly Father will also forgive you. But if you do not forgive men their trespasses, neither will your Father forgive your trespasses."

The Flourishing Way describes forgiveness as no longer "feeling angry or resentful toward someone for an offense, flaw, or mistake." A lot of times we get confused about what forgiveness is. It is a choice to not stay angry. It doesn't mean you have to forget. The offense happened. But allowing anger to control your life is poison for your soul.

A quote I saw on Pinterest nails the topic of forgiveness:

> *Forgive. Let go of your anger and disappointment. Do not worry about getting even. Do not hold onto bitterness and resentment. When you hold on to anger about the past, you only hurt yourself. Forgiveness does not mean what they did was right or justified; it means that you no longer punish yourself with sadness and frustration for what they did. It means you accept the past for what it is, so that you can move forward. It might be hard to forgive sometimes, but it is much harder to keep carrying the weight of anger.*

I love this so much because it is true. When you hold on to unforgiveness, you are punishing yourself. That person who offended you is out and about, not even thinking about it anymore. They are out living their best life, not thinking about you. They have moved on. You should move on too.

Pride prevents us from forgiving

A couple of days ago at work, I got into an altercation with a coworker. I came home and was so hurt by someone's words. I really struggled with how I was going to handle it. Then the Lord reminded me of this book,

MY MESS, HIS GRACE!

and I thought about what I would tell you to do in this situation. Obviously, I would want you to let it go and move on. But when you're heated, lots of scenarios run through your mind, such as *I should have said XYZ or I should done XYZ.* If you can picture it, I had an angel on one shoulder and a demon on the other shoulder. I let that go on for a good five hours. What the heck was I thinking? I let this steal my joy for five hours of my day. Why? Pride. I believe pride is the reason we do not want to forgive by nature.

Let's talk a little bit about pride. Proverbs 13:10 says, "By pride comes nothing but strife. But with well-advised is wisdom." When we choose to not forgive (let go), we are choosing to stand in pride and not in wisdom. I am very thankful the Lord spoke to me. I had to humble myself and make a decision to not be mad. I wondered how this was going to go down at work tomorrow. After praying about it, I felt like the Lord was saying to just let it go and be normal, to act as if nothing happened. So that's what I did. Guess what? That was wisdom in full-blown manifestation. We both were fine and actually my coworker embraced what he had originally been resisting. Maybe he did that because guys more easily let things go. They can have a full-blown fight with another guy and then be fine the next day, whereas we girls tend to hold on and get in our heads over a situation.

I would have held on to it if the Lord hadn't reminded me to let go of my pride. Pride has a very sneaky way of creeping in and controlling our thoughts, will, and emotions, which leads to unforgiveness, which leads to bitterness, which leads to illness. See how crafty the enemy is! We don't even see it happening at the time. Have you ever thought you forgave someone or something, but two months later, you still feel heated talking about it? That is pride holding on to that offense.

Proverbs 16:18 says, "Pride goes before destruction, and a haughty spirit before a fall."

The Webster dictionary describes haughty as "blatantly and disdainfully proud: having or showing an attitude of superiority and contempt for people or things perceived to be inferior."

These are very harsh but real descriptions of pride and haughty. Can you think of someone you know that really wears unforgiveness and pride like it's their prerogative? They are proud to be proud! How do you feel when you are around them? How do you feel when you leave their presence? Do you feel drained? Do you feel negative? Do you feel turned off? This is how unforgiveness seeps out of the pores. The Bible tells us in Matthew 12:34, "Out of the abundance of the heart the mouth speaks." We need to be conscious of what comes out of our mouths. We can take a real inventory of what is in our hearts. Then we need to ask God to help us forgive and clean out our hearts and begin a *new* work in us.

The problems with unforgiveness

When it comes to forgiveness, please try to keep at the forefront of your mind that unforgiveness equals poison. We don't want to poison our minds. We wouldn't go and drink a bottle of poison and think we'll be okay. We know if we drink a bottle of poison, we are going to die very shortly. When we drink the poison of unforgiveness, we are killing our spirits. Remember those old ladies who are bitter? Let's choose to not be bitter and embrace forgiveness.

Have you ever been to a gathering where two of the guests haven't forgiven each other? Everyone else that was invited feels uncomfortable because those two are there. You might absolutely love and adore those two, but the dynamics are so stressful you can cut it with a knife. When we choose to not forgive, we make everyone around us feel like they are walking on eggshells. How sad is that? Now we are making others suffer because our pride will not allow us to forgive and let go. This isn't fair to anyone. Again, you don't have to feel warm and fuzzy toward the person who offended you. But when you forgive them and you are at peace, you won't have that tension in the air where unforgiveness is. Your innocent friends and family will be grateful you forgave and didn't carry that unforgiveness to their daughter's wedding or Thanksgiving dinner.

As you can imagine, I have been in many of these scenarios with my mom and ex-husband. My mom and I obviously have the same family. My ex-husband and I have children together. There have been many family gatherings where we had to bite our tongues and stay away from each other. Neither one of us was going to miss out on a family function. That didn't make sense.

If we missed out, then it wasn't fair to our children or other family members. So we went. But let me tell you, it was much easier when forgiveness was given. We have long since passed the tension part. But for a while, we wouldn't say "hi" to each other, or if we did say "hi," that was all we said. Then we avoided each other like the plague. I would be on one side, and he would be on the other side of the get-together. Because of our tension, we couldn't both be around someone at the same time. Just awkward. This is a great reason alone to forgive.

This was hard on me because I love to be happy and goofy. But when your heart is pounding and you feel anxious in an environment, that is hard to do. You can't be yourself. So when I was living in unforgiveness, I would find myself getting quiet and withdrawing whenever my mom or ex was around before I had forgiven them. That isn't normal Kristie. So when I realized I didn't like the way I felt around the offender, I decided I wanted joy more than unforgiveness. Choosing forgiveness freed me to be myself—who I actually like by the way.

God sees the good

In Luke 7:40–50 Jesus talks about forgiving the sinful woman:

And Jesus answered and said to Simon. "Simon, I have something to say to you." So he said, "Teacher say it." There was a certain creditor who had two debtors. One owed five hundred denarii, and the other fifty. And when they had nothing at which to repay, he freely forgave them both. Tell me, which of them will love him more? Simon answered and said, "I suppose the one whom he forgave more." And He said to him "You have rightly judged." Then he turned to the woman and said to Simon. "Do you see this woman? I entered your house; you gave Me no water for My feet, but she has washed my feet with her tears and wiped them with the hair of her head." "You gave Me no kiss, but this woman has not ceased to kiss My feet since the time I came in. You did not anoint My head with oil, but this woman has anointed My feet with fragrant oil. Therefore I say to you, her sins, which are many, are forgiven, for she loved much. But to whom little is forgiven, the same loves little." Then He said to her, "Your sins are forgiven." And those who sat at the table with Him began to say to themselves, "Who is this who even forgives sins?" Then He said to the woman, "Your faith has saved you. Go in peace."

This is amazing. We have all sinned and fallen short of God's glory. It may seem like a little sin or a huge sin. But God doesn't have a barometer with a line saying your sins are too high so He can't forgive you. God is not in a box. He sees us through His eyes. That passage says her sins are many, but somehow God's love for her is still huge. He saw the good in her, and He protected her from Simon's hurtful words. Simon wanted to shame her. But God said *no*! Jesus pointed out the good in her. I believe God does the same with us. He sees the good in us.

Are you harboring unforgiveness toward yourself? Sister friend, please don't. You are only hurting yourself. God sees you through His eyes, just like He did this woman. He sees the good in you. He knows your heart. Please take some time to reflect on your life. Reflect on God's love. Speak truth to yourself. The enemy would love for you to not feel worthy of God's grace and forgiveness. But the enemy is a liar!

There is no sin too big for God to forgive and redeem you. Please journal below and pour your heart out to God like the woman did when she cried at Jesus's feet. He is waiting, and He loves you so much!

Journal Notes

Journal Notes

Chapter 6

Hope

When bills come in faster than you can blink an eye, your children are struggling in different areas, or you're getting random trials coming your way and you do not know how you are going to come up for air, that's when we need to have hope that God is in control, and He wants what is best for us. When these times happened, which was often, I would pray "God, please call the dogs off of me," meaning tell the enemy no more. Pleeeaaasse!! God was always faithful to answer. The peace would come almost instantly. God always knows what we need before we pray for it. He is just waiting for us to turn to Him in times of need.

And when we do, there is hope. He will not forsake us and will often send us signs that He is watching over us.

Doves, dimes, and butterflies

When I was thirty years old, my grandpa went to be with Jesus. I have been a grandpa's girl since I could remember. To me, he was perfect. I worshipped the ground he walked on. He loved Jesus wholeheartedly, and I remember him sitting at the kitchen table, reading his Bible, and praying in the mornings. He was so faithful when it came to spending time with the Lord. The example he set for me will forever be embedded in my heart.

Psalms 1:1–3 (NKJ) was his favorite passage:

Blessed is the man who walks not in the counsel of the wicked (ungodly), nor stands in the path of sinners. Nor sits in the seat of the scornful; But his delight is in the law of the Lord, And in His law he meditates day and night. He shall be like a tree planted by rivers of water, That brings forth its fruit in its season. Whose leaf also shall not wither; and whatever he does shall prosper.

This scripture is what my grandpa lived out. He was always in God's word and kept himself in fellowship. I remember he would never let me come and go without anointing my head with oil and praying over me. I knew God loved me when I was blessed with my grandparents. The bond my grandpa and I had was very strong. He called me the apple of his eye, and I called him Bompa because when I was little I couldn't say "grandpa," and it just stuck. Grandpa would always join Grandma, my brother, my cousins, and me when we would go clothing shopping. Talk about the patience of a saint.

I remember our Friday nights with Grandpa. We would order pizza, go to Kmart to buy our favorite black licorice ropes, and then go to the store and buy ice cream. Our last stop would be to pick up the pizza we ordered, then go home and watch *Love Boat* and *Fantasy Island* and pig out.

Saturday morning he would take us to the park while he played horseshoes, and he would let us ride our little bikes there and back. He was the kind of grandpa that had an unwavering love for his grandkids.

I had so many amazing memories with the best grandpa in the world. So, you can imagine how heartbroken I was when he went to be with the Lord. I had never felt my heart break like that before. I didn't know that kind of hurt existed. It took me quite a while to get to where I wouldn't break down crying by looking at his picture or thinking of something with him in it.

The day my grandpa passed away I was standing in the kitchen looking out the window when I saw a dove sitting on the corner of my lawn just watching me. That same dove came back every day for months. I remember telling my mother-in-law about the dove, and she said, "That is your grandpa letting you know he is with the Lord and he is good." Just last week twenty years later, I went outside and a dove was sitting on my lawn looking at me. I have been going through a lot, and I knew that was God's way of saying He hasn't forgotten me. God is with me, and He has me in the palm of his hands.

God is so faithful to speak to us. We just need to listen and pay attention to our surroundings. God wants to love on us and encourage us. One of my favorite things to ask God is "Please love on me today." He always comes through. I try to remember when I ask that, so when I get that sweet text, phone call, or a compliment from a friend or loved one, I know that was God loving on me.

When my mother-in-law was battling cancer, I kept finding dimes everywhere. This was a very trying time for me. My husband was having an affair, and I was taking care of three children by myself because he worked nights. When he was home, he wasn't really home. He was checked out. But these dimes showed up whenever I felt defeated and like there was no hope. When my sister-in-law and I were going on a walk, I shared the story of the dimes with her. Lo and behold, she had kept finding dimes everywhere also. My father-in-law said when God gives us dimes that is His way of telling us that everything is going to be okay.

I remember holding on to my father-in-law's words like they were gold. For twenty years now, I have found dimes at the most needed times. When finances were tight, I would find a dime and I would know everything would be okay. When the kids would act up, I would find a dime and I would know everything was going to be okay again. One time, I thought everything was going well when I found a whole pile of dimes in the parking lot. I thought, *Why? Everything is going so well.* Shortly after that things got crazy, and I remembered the pile of dimes. God let me know that everything would be okay in advance. Now it was getting real!

The best part of finding dimes was telling the kids that God has everything under control so everything would be okay. This taught them to trust God. Now as adults, they know God can use whatever He wants to comfort them, and they love dimes too. It's like what the Bible verse Proverbs 22:6 promises us: "Train up a child in the way he should go, and when he is old he will not depart from it."

I love this verse. When my first child was born, my aunt bought me a plaque with a train on it with this verse. It stayed with me for thirty-one years.

When my mother-in-law died of cancer, my heart was broken. I had the best mother-in-law a girl could ask for. She was the most loving, giving lady. She loved her grandbabies so much. She was selfless and had a servant's heart. Looking back, I see how much she sacrificed for all of us.

At first, I was a bit lost when she died. Who would call us to tell us goodnight? Who would I go visit at night when I got off work? Who would I talk to that would keep my secrets? But then, I kept seeing white butterflies everywhere. Again, I told my sister-in-law, and she had been seeing them everywhere also. We both laughed and said, "Oh, Juerra (my mother-in-law's nickname) is with us." It is the sweetest thing because now when I see butterflies, I can't help but think she is with us and God is loving on me. Today twenty years later, I went for a small twenty-minute walk, and this white butterfly stayed by me for a good amount of time. I had to video it and send it to my sister-in-law and my kids. You might be thinking, *Doves, dimes, and butterflies... really?* Well, this is what God has used with my family and me. It might be puppies for you. All I know is, I wholeheartedly believe God will use whatever and whomever He wants to show you He loves you, and He hasn't forgotten you! The enemy would like us to feel defeated, forgotten, and unloved. But God sent His son to die for us. Now that is *love* at the core!!

Having hope and trusting God

Romans 5:5 tells us "Now hope does not disappoint, because the love of God has been poured out into our hearts by the Holy Spirit who was given to us." Trusting and having hope in God

One thing I definitely learned over the years as a single, struggling mom is that God is always holding me in the palm of His hands. That is one thing I can keep my hope in: trusting that God has me. Over and over He has shown His mighty presence in my life and in the lives of those I love. He loves you, dear friend. He is holding you when you don't even realize it.

Recently the doctor found a mass in my uterus along with several growths, an enlarged uterus, and several cysts. In all of that, all I heard was "mass in the uterus." My first reaction was to cry. I thought, *I'm just starting to enjoy being a grandma of two amazing little boys, and I just found the love of my life. I don't want to go through this.* Like anyone ever wants to go through cancer or any health issues. I saw my life literally flash before my eyes and was quickly reminded that God has me now, just like He always has. I had to remember my hope is in God. I cannot put into words how I felt at the moment. I just knew that I needed to trust God and believe that whatever happens, God can use it for His good. That is the only thing that gave me peace.

Sometimes we need to ask the Lord to help us speak the truth to ourselves. The truth is if I did die, I would be with Jesus. If I lived, I would go through this medical process and then would have more downtime to write this book and spend time with Jesus. Then I realized, it's a win-win! I win in this because I get more Jesus either way. I've had the biopsy, and praise the Lord, it isn't cancer. However, I do need surgery. Guess what? I can have more time with Jesus and time to write while I'm down with the surgery. Also, all of the stuff growing in my uterus will be gone and won't be able to turn into cancer. It's a great win! Having hope in Christ brings forth resolution and peace of mind.

I'm not saying that trusting God and having hope in God is easy for everyone or was always easy for me. After going through so much in life and always being forced to lean on God for help, my grandma (my mom's mom), the one I lived with growing up, knew how to continue onward in hope. She was the best example of this. Life could be hectic, people could be hurt or sick, and she could have a family emergency and you name it, yet she always had a smile on her face. She would say, "All we can do is pray and trust that God has us."

If you're anything like I was, it was hard for me to just trust. My insides would be turned upside down and inside out because I needed to fix things. I'm a fixer. Telling a fixer to have hope or faith is like telling them to sit down and be quiet and don't move. Yeah . . . that doesn't work for me. So, as you can imagine, I had to go through many life trials to figure this one out. I'm not saying I have it mastered, but thank the Lord I'm better than I was.

In times of trial, you need to turn to God, trust Him, and have hope that things will work out for thy good. I asked my kids what gave them hope during our time together after the divorce. My daughter said, "When we would have our time together as a family unit such as dinner, walks, hikes, swimming, going to Arizona, etc. That's where I always felt hope. Heart."

This shows you can always find the good in the bad. If you focus more on the good, you will be better at having hope. After the trail of divorce, I learned that God speaks to us, He wants what is best for us, and He always provides. During our outings that my daughter mentioned, we would have so much fun. We would talk, joke, laugh, cry, and eat. I can see why it would give her hope that everything would be okay. These were amazing bonding times. God definitely can take what the enemy intended for harm and turn it into good. He grew hope in us during this season.

How is God working in your life? Is he developing hope in you? Take a moment to reflect on what lessons God is teaching you and journal what He shows you.

Journal Notes

Journal Notes

Chapter 7

Joy

Oxford languages definition of joy is "a feeling of great pleasure and happiness, 'tears of joy.'"

The Bible's definition of joy is "a feeling of good pleasure and happiness that is dependent on who Jesus is rather than on who we are or what is happening around us. Joy comes from the Holy Spirit, abiding in God's presence and from hope in His word."

In the book The Power of Joy, Nick Breau defines joy as "the roadmap for action-takers who want real change. It combines powerful tools and practical guidance that guarantees big transformation, inside and out."

In the Bible, Proverbs 8 tells us that God says this about Himself: "I was filled with delight day after day, rejoicing always in His presence, rejoicing in His whole world and delighting in mankind."

When we are going through life and hitting rough patches, we can forget that our joy comes from the Lord, and it is powerful.

My story

I work in the medical field, and during COVID-19, it was a crazy time. The uncertainty that we all lived through will go down in history for sure. Coworkers and patients walked through the hospital corridors with their heads down and stopped saying good morning and goodnight. I can only imagine what they were facing at home. Their spouse might have had to work from home or could have been out of a job for a while, causing an extreme amount of burden and stress. Loved ones were in the hospital sick with Covid and getting worsening symptoms. Many manufacturers were back-ordered so we either couldn't order our supplies in time or they would be stuck on boats with no one to unload them, all while patients needed our care. This list can go on and on. Yes, it was a hard time. But we could still find joy. How did you find joy during this time?

My first grandchild was born during COVID-19, and her mom was only allowed to have one person with her in the hospital during labor. I work in the same hospital where my daughter gave birth, and I couldn't even send food to them. This was extremely hard. I was anxious because I am a hands-on mom and grandma, kind of like a mama bear. My kids will tell you this is putting it mildly. They could tell you stories.

Despite these hardships, I found joy. I was able to have some amazing time with the Lord, through devotions, prayer, worship and just being silent before God.

My Mess, His Grace!

Joy comes to us in many ways. My children and grandchildren bring me so much joy. I love being around them, texting them, and talking with them on the phone. I also get a lot of joy out of FaceTiming them. I thank God for technology. We don't get to see each other in person every day, but we can FaceTime and that helps a lot. I'm very blessed that my children allow me to watch the boys when they want a date or get away. I cherish those times with the boys so much. Sometimes if I'm having a stressful day, I will look at the baby's pictures and ask God to help me. I instantly feel joy pouring back into my heart.

When I'm hiking, riding my bike, camping, or going to the beach and just being outdoors, I find joy. I feel like a child just absorbing the fresh air and exploring. I get giddy when I'm out on hikes. It is just the coolest thing for me.

Yesterday I had surgery and couldn't really do a whole lot. My daughter and my grandson came over to bring us dinner. Do you know how hard it is to not pick up a twenty-month-old whom you adore, and who wants you to hold him? I couldn't resist. I held him a few times. He just melts my heart. He calls me Bom Bom. So with his big brown eyes and cute smile, I couldn't resist. I'm sore now. But he just brings me so much joy, I couldn't say no.

Choosing joy

What do you do when you feel like your joy is depleted? This is important. A lot of people don't know how to turn off what is weighing them down. They can fall into a slump of feeling down. I want to encourage you to find what brings you joy that can pull you out of any slump. What puts a smile on your face? Practice running to God and asking Him for help and doing that thing that puts a smile on your face. I promise you will have joy poured into your spirit, and your mood will change.

Joy is a choice. We can choose to be down or choose joy in most situations. When life throws us curve balls, it's easy to fall into the pit of sorrow. Whenever I let sorrow take over, it feels heavy and draining. But if I choose to take the high road to joy instead, I feel light and happy. Sometimes we have to ask ourselves if we really want to feel down and sorrowful. As soon as we tell ourselves "no absolutely not," we can snap out of it. That's where the choice comes in. We have to remind ourselves that we do have a choice in how we feel and how we respond. Our reaction is what will lead us to how we feel internally.

We have to wake up and realize the old patterns that didn't work won't bring new results. We need to make choices for change that will help us grow and feel joyful. I'm not talking about fake happiness. I'm talking about Holy Spirit–filled joy. I believe the Lord always allows us to be stretched so we can grow. We need to put aside that spirit of pride and hear what God is trying to teach us.

My kids will tell you I have a tough love mindset. I'm nurturing as well, so there is a balance. However, I am a big fan of the phrase "turn that frown upside down." Life is too short to be unhappy. God has *big* plans for each and every one of us. If we spend our short time here on this Earth constantly unhappy, we will miss the mark. I just watched a YouTube video by Tom Bilyeu called "Overcoming self-doubt." Tom makes a few statements that really resonated with me on this topic.

- We need to intentionally reject certain thoughts.
- We need to decide what we are going to pursue mentally.
- We become what we repeat.

If we are constantly focusing on the negative things, then that is where we will stay. I have Post-it notes up at work on my monitor with acronyms to remind me when situations arise. For example, I have a Post-it note that says DLTEUY, which means "don't let the enemy use you."

So when I get a cranky coworker or customer, I read that, and it helps me with rejecting negative thoughts and deciding where I want to go mentally. This helps me a great deal. You will want to find what works for you. This just works for me.

Surround yourself with people who choose joy

Sometimes certain people in your life do not chase joy. I'm not a licensed counselor; however, I have counseled many young ladies over the years. Nothing is harder than giving someone Godly counsel and them not wanting it. They keep coming back for more counsel, but they don't want to follow your advice. It is the craziest thing to me. Would you rather be unhappy in your situation? Would you rather go round and round in what hurts you? If your friends and loved ones stay in the sorrow, then unfortunately, you need to let those people go and figure life out without them. They are choosing the sorrowful draining route. They aren't choosing joy. They are like a cat chasing their tail, and you don't have to chase the tail with them.

A while back, a young lady would call me daily asking for prayer. It took me a while to realize that she didn't want a prayer, she just wanted someone to listen. The problem was she didn't want to change. It was almost like she enjoyed being sad and stuck in her situation. It didn't matter how many different ways I would shed light on making things look positive, she wasn't ready. This is hard for me to wrap my mind around. If I come to you and ask you for prayer and you give me ideas of how to make a change for the better, I'm all-in. It actually got to a point when one of my boys told me, "Mom, you need to stop trying to help her. She doesn't want help." How did I not recognize that? I was getting drained and tired every time I talked to her

My Mess, His Grace!

because it was like a no-win situation. Nothing I said or did would look positive to that young lady because she chose the road to sorrow over the road to joy.

These people can drain you, while those who are filled with joy can help you choose joy. Joy is contagious. Do you have a friend or friends that whenever you're around them, you leave filled with joy? Whenever I'm with my children, they make me laugh a big portion of the time. They have a way of making most situations fun. Even when it's a serious engagement, it can be turned into a happy time of fellowship. The important thing is to not stay stuck in a sorrowful place. Allow yourself to seek a joyful mentality and reject the thoughts that want to hold you down.

Take a moment to reflect on how you think. Are there negative thoughts that replay in your heart and mind that keep you from God's fullness of joy? What will you do from today forward to reject those thoughts and change your mindset? Journal below and come back as often as you need to remind yourself.

Journal Notes

Journal Notes

Chapter 8

Perseverance

My story

The day before my twenty-first birthday, I was starting a new job in downtown Los Angeles. It was 5:00 a.m. and still dark out, the rain was pouring, and I was in bumper-to-bumper traffic in my 1988 tiny burgundy Hyundai Excel Hatchback. While I was in the slow lane, getting ready to exit Martin Luther King Jr. Boulevard, a car two cars ahead of me blew out one of his tires, causing the school bus driver in front of me to slam on her brakes. When she did that, the bus drifted toward the left lane and crashed into the front of my car.

I cried out to God, "Don't let me get hurt." I'm not sure why that was the first thing to come to mind. But I genuinely meant it. I couldn't pull over to the shoulder lane because my car wasn't drivable. When I leaned down to grab my purse, it wasn't there. I was so dazed and confused and in complete shock. I wasn't

MY MESS, HIS GRACE!

sure what had just happened, but thankfully, a lot of witnesses pulled over to offer assistance.

A lady came and got me out of the car and asked me if I was okay. As I stood outside the car in the pouring rain, I stared at my car that looked like a crushed soda can. The car just folded, yet I didn't even have a scratch on me. That was amazing. I had survived a major car accident.

The tow truck driver towed me and my wrecked Hyundai to my new job. It was the closest place to where we were. Thankfully, my new boss was also my old boss, so she knew me on a personal level and knew I wasn't being irresponsible. Plus, she saw my car when the tow truck brought it into the parking lot.

My aunt who has always been there for me called AAA and had them tow me and my damaged car home, which was an hour away. My aunt met us at my house and brought me one of her cars to borrow until I could get my car situated so I had transportation to get to my new job.

As soon as I walked into my house, my landline was ringing (this was before cell phones). The city of Los Angeles was offering immediate assistance. My car insurance company at the time sent me to a lawyer, and before I knew it, the day was gone, and I was feeling some soreness. The shock was wearing off, and reality was settling in.

I remember going to see the lawyer, and, of course, they wanted me to sue the city of Los Angeles. I told her, "I'm a Christian and we do not sue anyone." God will take care of me. God will provide. Well, Praise God, He did. The attorney talked me into allowing the city to pay for my doctor's and chiropractor's visits. This was a huge blessing because even though I didn't have a scratch on me, I was sore and stiff, so I needed the adjustments. The visits to the chiropractor lasted a year. It started off every day, then moved to every other day, to once a week, and then tapered from there.

When I remember this time, I see how God answered my cry to not let me get hurt. He didn't allow me to lose my life or have any life-threatening damage. But he also allowed me to go through the chiropractor visits, which reminded me every time that I was thankful to be alive and that God had been right there protecting me.

I could have chosen to feel sorry for myself and think, "I'm out of a car, I have a sore back and neck, I'm getting migraines, and God didn't protect me," but I remembered what that car looked like, and I chose to believe that God had saved my life.

Choose a positive outlook

Have you ever been in a life-threatening situation? How did you react? These are key moments to reflect on and see how God was right there protecting you. It might not be in the way you would think, but His thinking and ways are so different from ours.

Isaiah 55:8–9 says, "For my thoughts are not your thoughts, neither are your ways my ways says the Lord. For the heavens are higher than the earth, So are my ways higher than your ways, And my thoughts than your thoughts."

How we look at situations and how we react to them are the important parts. If you have a hard time looking at things with a glass-half-full mentality, seeing the good in every situation, I encourage you to practice looking at things differently. We go through trials in our lives to help mold and shape us. If we don't have a good reaction this time, it's okay. We can learn from it and have a better reaction the next time.

I'm not saying that choosing to look at situations with a positive outlook is always easy. I'm fifty-three years old and have learned this along the way. But I can tell you I have a lot of peace when I choose to be joyful in these trying situations.

I recently had an ah-ha moment! I've read this scripture countless times, and it literally just hit me. This is what God means when he says in James 1:2, "My brethren count it all joy when you fall into various trials, knowing that the testing of our faith produces patience." So after fifty-three years of trials, I am now always patient. Just kidding. I have learned about patience, but more importantly, I've learned to choose joy.

My daughter's fiance asked my daughter, "Why doesn't your mom stress?" I thought that was hilarious. I don't stress because I don't want to stress. You see I spent a good portion of my life stressing over things that God had control of anyway. But losing sleep and having a racing mind and heart are not worth it—joy is. So choose joy.

Choosing to persevere

What is perseverance to you? To me, it's when you keep on keeping on to weather the storms of life. Life can be brutal for everyone. Yes, some people have it harder than others, but we all experience trials.

Romans 5:3–5 says, "And not only that, but we also glorify in tribulations, knowing that tribulation produces perseverance; and perseverance, character; and character hope. Now hope doesn't disappoint, because the love of God has been poured out into our hearts by the Holy Spirit who was given to us."

People by nature would rather take the easy way out. It seems easier and less painful. Unfortunately, that isn't always so because when we take the easy way out, we miss out on the blessings that come from the finished product. I'm sure you have all heard of the analogy of the diamond. When a diamond is found either in the ground or in a rock, they are usually rough and not shaped. But once the diamond is cut and polished, it is beautiful.

Just like baking a cake. You wouldn't eat the flour, baking powder, raw egg, salt, or vanilla by itself and say, "yummy!" It isn't until the cake has gone through the entire recipe, mixing process, and baking process, that it will taste delicious. It's the same with us. We have to go through the yucky-tasting things in life and persevere before we can come out looking polished.

Those trials in life make us who we are to become. It can be hard to wrap our minds around why bad situations happen to us. I was a single mom for many years and would often ask God why He would want me to do this alone. I finally realized that I wasn't alone. I had God first and foremost, but I also had an army of amazing women in my life that I call family. Now that I am an empty nester, I can see why God had me raise my children as a single mom. They would have had such a different upbringing if I had raised them with their dad. Not to toot my own horn, but toot toot. Okay, that was meant to be funny. I am so proud of how my children turned out. They love God, family, and life. I am so glad I stuck through the hardships of being a single mom.

What is your first reaction when you're in a difficult situation and you have the choice to run or stick it out? I know for me, I rationalize why I should leave or quit. I can conjure up a whole list of reasons to not stick something out. The problem with not sticking it out is you will never finish what you started. My daughter once pointed this out to me. She didn't know how much I needed to hear the words "Mom, you never finish what you start." Okay, I don't know about you, but I can be pretty competitive. So to me, this was a challenge. She was right, though. I would jump from MLM to MLM, trying to find my home. The problem with that is there are always going to be upsides and downsides to every business. So I decided it was time to stay right where I was and stick it out. Wouldn't you know it, friends from different companies just started popping up out of nowhere to introduce me to new ventures. They all sounded amazing; however, I needed to finish what I had started with the company I was with.

What about bigger decisions? If you're in an unhealthy marriage or have an unhealthy friendship, what should you do? Should you persevere and stick it out? No, that is not what I am saying. But there is a huge difference between being in an unhealthy relationship or friendship and just being unhappy and finding it difficult to stick it out. If you are unhappy, you can work on it. You can persevere through that. So you need to assess whether you are just unhappy and don't want to deal with the difficult parts or whether you are unhappy because the relationship isn't healthy. My friend Laura told me years ago, "If a relationship doesn't bring you closer to God, then it's not from God." This saying has come to my mind so many times over the last twenty years. Marriage is a covenant between you, God, and your husband. So an unhealthy relationship does not bring you closer to God. While being unhappy isn't a good reason to quit, if the relationship is unhealthy, then that's another story altogether. So too with any major relationship and decision in life. You should be in prayer and mindful of the relationships and situations you are in that you want to quit that you really should stick out. If you're supposed to do it, if it's right for you, then you need to stick it out no matter how hard it may be at times.

When it comes to tasks we have committed to, we do sometimes overcommit and need to take things off our plates. Only you and God know what those things are. But if it is a legal obligation or something you feel called to do. God won't change His mind and say, "Just kidding. You can quit that now." God is the same yesterday, today, and forever. He doesn't change His mind. That is our fleshly nature.

Part of working through perseverance means being content with what you have in front of you. We are often looking for the next best thing. We think, "Oh, this idea, thing, or opportunity looks more appealing to me." My friend, just because it looks better doesn't mean it is meant for you.

Choose to be content with what you have. Choose to commit to all healthy choices you have made, all the tasks that are right for you, and all relationships and situations that are healthy, and persevere and see them through when times get tough.

Persevering through God's timing

God is always looking out for our best interests, and He always holds us in His hands. I believe He was holding me during the major car accident, and that's why I walked away without a scratch. He was holding me during all of those MLM adventures, probably shaking his head, saying, "No, don't do it." But I kept doing them. God allowed me to go through those seasons so I would come out realizing where He was in the midst of my poor decisions along with unforeseen circumstances. He doesn't look at us and think, "You fool. I told you not to do that." That is condemnation. God doesn't condemn us. That is what the enemy does.

God is gracious and gently leads us and reminds us that He has our back. The Bible tells us in Proverbs 13:12, "Hope deferred makes the heart sick, But when the desire comes it is the tree of life." Have you ever waited on God to answer your prayer, and it just seemed like it was never going to happen? Well, my friend, you are not alone. I can write an entire book on the subject of waiting on God. Like my friend Rina said to me all those years ago, "God has not forgotten you." Well, He has not forgotten you either.

This morning when I was on my way to work, I felt the Lord ask me to be very vulnerable with you and share what I struggled with in the quietness of my own home. I had somehow mastered wearing a mask, as I was just fine the way I was in my singleness. I would go through the motions of my day-to-day tasks—go to church, attend my kids' sporting events, etc.—and smile and say, "I'm doing great." When in my heart, I was broken. I couldn't understand why God was blessing other people with long healthy marriages and new relationships that flourished. Meanwhile, I was watching these relationships with people I was very close to and wondering, "What about me, God?" Everyone tells you the Christianeese answers like, "Seek God first and He will bless you," "God doesn't like women to be single moms," "He will bring you someone fast," "You're beautiful, so you will meet someone soon." That list can go on and on. But the truth was, while I had to share my children with their dad, my heart was broken. I felt alone but didn't want anyone to know how alone and sad I really was.

When my kids would go to their dad's, I would spend the day with just God and me. These were beautiful times looking back. But let me tell you, I would wrestle with God. I would lay it on thick and cry out, "Why is this happening to me? Why do I have to share my kids? How long are you going to keep me single? When am I going to get up for air financially? I know you said you haven't forgotten me, but I feel forgotten." I would cry, yell, and sometimes scream at God. I sincerely felt like I was reaping what he sowed. This went on for many years.

During this season of singleness, I made some very poor choices. I was on a spiritual roller coaster. I would be really close to the Lord one minute, then running in the wrong direction the next. I didn't know how to rein in my emotions and frustrations. I just didn't want to be lonely anymore. When my kids were home, I was happy. But when they went to their dad's, I would feel how alone I really was. It didn't matter how busy I kept myself that lonely, left-out feeling would rear its ugly head.

God's timing is perfect. I know we have all heard that one before. Hindsight looking back, I know this to be true in my case. I was a single mom from 2003 to 2019. In 2017 my oldest went into the Navy. In 2019 my youngest went into the Army. I was with my daughter until 2021. I am now forever grateful to God that He allowed me to be a single mom. If I had stayed in that marriage, our children wouldn't be who they are today, and they are pretty awesome. Since I stayed single during all the child-rearing years, I was able to raise them with the Lord without the influence of anyone else. It was just me and the Lord. They are all thriving in their lives and have blessed me with two beautiful grandsons. Now that they are grown, the Lord has blessed me with a good companion.

I want to encourage you to stick it out. With that thing or relationship that you're ready to quit, figure out if it is of God, and if it is, stick it out. If you're waiting for a blessing from Him, continue to wait in patience, knowing his timing is perfect. If you stick to your commitments and wait in patience, you will be blessed in the end. God has not forgotten you! Take time to journal below about what you're wanting to quit. Ask God to give you discernment and really seek Him on this subject.

Journal Notes

Journal Notes

Chapter 9

Road To Healing

We have talked about some of my ideas on forgiveness, but let's talk about the aftermath of hurtful events.

My story

The effects of the affair brought on anxiety, depression, other stresses, self-blame, self-shame, obsessive thoughts, insecurities, and PTSD. But it wasn't all my husband's fault. You see, I wasn't perfect. Just because he was the one who had the affair didn't mean I had it all together. I needed to work on myself as well.

At that time, I really struggled with thoughts of negativity about myself. I thought I wasn't good enough, pretty enough, nice enough, or worthy of love. Even before the affair, my husband hadn't spent much time with me. He always had his own plans with other people that didn't include me. My biological dad never wanted to spend time with me, so I believed that I wasn't worthy of a man's attention or friendship. I didn't feel like my mom liked me, let alone loved me. The affair just put the icing on the cake to this insecurity of nobody likes or wants me.

In order to heal from this, I had to choose to heal and take action.

While I loved reading before all of this affair stuff, reading afterward became my lifeline. There are so many gifted authors out there that have been through what you have been through. One way God healed me was through His gifted authors.

I became obsessed with the Bible Book Store and Barnes & Noble. I would pray and ask God to lead me to the book or books that He wanted me to get. I was determined to get healed. So I would focus on the area that I was struggling in—whether it was forgiveness, lacking joy, single parenting, having hope, and so on—and look for books on the area. I would sit on the floor and read the back of the book and the reviews, then I would buy the book that spoke to me the most at the time. So pretty frequently, I would load my three kids in the car and say, "Let's go to the bookstore." They loved it because they were able to pick out a book for themselves.

Reading was only one part of my healing process. I also leaned into my family for support. This meant I had to open up. An insecure person opening up when they feel hurt is challenging. I've never been one to open up too easily. But if I feel like you are a safe person, I will. (This is one reason I put off writing this book for twenty years: it required me to open up.) Hearing other peoples' stories and opinions was very overwhelming for me. I would literally shut down.

One day, long before the affair, God put it in my heart to have what my family calls "Family Fellowship." We would get together one day a month and fellowship, share, pray for each other, and eat. This was so pivotal for me. During "Family Fellowship," I was able to see that I wasn't the only one going through life's many trials. We were all facing situations. We were able to lock arms and really be there for each other and help each other. They helped me to acknowledge that my feelings were valid and that with God all things are possible.

Ways to heal

When you're in the trenches of your trial, it is hard, and you need to make a continuous effort to take action toward your own healing process.

Journaling: When you write things down and are honest with yourself, the visual brings your soul some sort of release. For me, journaling also helped me release my hurt, anger, and frustrations and document my challenges, goals, accomplishments, and things I was thankful for. Making goals and being thankful are huge parts of getting healthier.

Hobbies: Hobbies can help you stop overthinking. If you have any hobbies or would like to pick up one, I would encourage you to do so. I really didn't have any hobbies because my children were in sports, so I was busy with that. I guess you can say my kids were my hobby. Some of my single-mom friends would get a side business as a hobby, or go to one of those paint and wine nights. I have always wanted to go to one of those. Maybe one day soon. You have so many hobbies to choose from, so check out your options. If your friend invites you to an outing, go and enjoy yourself. Meet new friends, and you will find what works for you.

Staying active: This also helps you to stop overthinking. The kids and I would go for walks at night and hikes on the weekends before or after sports. We loved hiking, and now, it is so cool to see my older two adult children taking their little ones for walks. Something about exercise and fresh air is very freeing. Exercising also comes with many health benefits: controlling your weight, reducing heart disease, managing blood sugar, improving your sleep, reducing depression, and giving you mental energy and emotional wellness, which help to improve your mood. When you are out walking by yourself, I encourage you to thank God for His many blessings. Because despite the current trial, we should be thanking Him for many things. If walking by yourself doesn't sound appealing to you, you can get a walking buddy.

Engage in healthy friendships: My neighbor Buffy became my friend, and eventually, we considered each other family. One day I was out watching my children play and Buffy was outside watching her girls play.

My Mess, His Grace!

That is how we met. Coincidentally, I moved into the apartment right across from her apartment, and we discovered that our girls were on the same club soccer team. Her daughter Kylie went to try out for the team my daughter was on, and that's when our friendship started. When Buffy was sitting on the steps in front of her apartment reading her Bible, I knew this was a God thing. We would go to tournaments together and help each other split the costs, which was a huge help when the games were far away. We would rent a hotel, bring food, and cheer our girls on. Buffy and I would go for walks, and she would sometimes do a slow jog while I walked. I couldn't run because I thought I would rather die. Haha. These walks with Buffy were healing times for me. I met another single mom who understood me and the challenges I was facing.

Disengage from unhealthy friendships: Be careful who you surround yourself with. Friendships can be tricky. I learned this in my healing process. A lot of people are out for themselves. Those types of friends can be draining and take away from your healing process. Like the Bible tells us in Proverbs 27:17, "As iron sharpens iron, So a man sharpens the countenance of his friend." Your friendships should be like-minded. You should both be compatible with each other. I've had several good and not-so-good friends. If you feel like you're tired and drained after leaving a conversation or visit, it might not be the healthy friendship God wants you to have. You will need to pray and use discernment for clarity in your friendships.

The wrong friendships can feed your spirit with gunk. The right friendships should thrive. I have had some friendships that seemed good, but now that we have grown apart, I can see where it wasn't a healthy friendship. This is important because the wrong friendships can stunt the growth of your healing process. So you must be careful who you allow in your circle. I'm not saying live in fear and with a wall up. I just want you to be careful so you aren't wasting your healing time with people who aren't mindful of your needs.

Sisters in Christ, this also goes for your church friends. Just because you met your girlfriend at church, doesn't mean she is the best friend for you or vice versa. This is where the enemy can trip us up. I've grown close to many friends from church and have also been hurt by a handful. There are many real true, genuine Godly women out there that will have your best interest at heart. That is where prayer and discernment are very important. We need to remember we are living in a fallen world, and we all have our own issues.

Be a friend to others: Being a good friend is also a huge part of the healing process. When you can openly be your true self with a friend and listen to them when they speak, you can help them resolve their issues. This is healing for you also. Giving of ourselves with a generous heart is so healing, especially when you give without wanting anything in return. I'm not talking about money. I'm talking about when your friend needs you to just listen. That is what you do: just listen. When they need advice, then prayerfully give advice. If they just need to get out of the house and have dinner, then go to dinner.

Healing can come in surprising ways

I can't carry a tune to save my life, but soon after my divorce, I sang "Before He Cheats" by Carrie Underwood at karaoke night at my aunt's restaurant. Well, as you can imagine, this song really resonated with me. For some reason, I decided it would be a great idea to go into full-blown acting mode. I decided on a whim to put on a show for my family that was there and with a bunch of strangers.

I acted out each thing that the song says she did to get revenge: "dug my key into the side of his pretty little souped-up four-wheel drive, carved my name into his leather seats, took a Louisville slugger to both of his headlights." I have no idea where this animated Kristie came from. All I can say is some people will never forget my animated, passionate karaoke to the song "Before He Cheats."

It has been nineteen years, and this story still makes me blush. This is probably not the best way to bring about healing. But wow! All I can say is I woke up feeling like the weight of the world was off my shoulders. I released everything that was hurting me through that crazy show I put on. I wasn't going up there to be funny, but people laughed and still laugh about this show. I didn't go up there to get healing, but God sure turned my shenanigans into a healing moment. When I look back, I am so grateful for God's grace, first of all, but also that He knows us better than we know ourselves. That show didn't surprise Him. Healing comes even when we aren't looking for it.

Take some time to pray about it, and ask the Lord to show you how much He loves you and where He would like you to start on your road to healing. Write in the journal section what the Lord says will help you with your healing and what you are thankful for.

Journal Notes

Journal Notes

Chapter 10

God Always Holds Us in His Hands

Have you ever been through something and thought, "Where was God when this happened to me?"

My story

When I found out about the affair, it was a Thursday. The next day I was supposed to go to a retreat getaway weekend my grandma had bought for me. Missing the retreat wasn't an option. Staying home wasn't going to change the situation. So I decided to still go to the retreat despite my world being in shambles. This retreat was amazing. I met a lot of lifelong friends there and, eventually, became part of their ministry for a season.

The ministry was geared toward praying over you in different sessions. Each session had a different team of prayer warriors that would pray over you, and they were all very unique and special. In one of the sessions, the prayer team did an exercise with me. They asked me to close my eyes, think of a certain time in my life, and ask God to show me where He was during that moment when I was alone and afraid. This was so cool. I could literally see that God was right there with me. This might sound out there to you. But I can tell you from experience, this was so healing for me to know that God was right there with me, even in the most difficult of times. There is something so surreal when you know God is by your side. Whenever a bad memory comes to my mind, I do that exercise, and God is quick to remind me, He was by my side during that time also.

People have commented to me over the years, and said things like "You are so strong." I am not strong. I am fragile and have had my heart torn to pieces by people I should trust. But God! God has poured into me and filled me up to handle the waves of life.

Remember God is there

We can go through the most difficult time in our lives and question, *Where was God? Does God love me? Why is He allowing this to happen? Why did He allow this person to pass away? Why, why, why?* These questions could keep going on forever. The truth is God doesn't want bad things to happen. But we live in a fallen world, and things happen. We will continue to experience trials until we are home with Jesus one day. That doesn't mean He left us. He wants us to trust in Him and believe

MY MESS, HIS GRACE!

that no matter what happens, He loves us. His love for us never changes. The Bible tells us in Deuteronomy 31:6, "Be strong and of good courage, do not fear nor be afraid of them; for the Lord your God. He is the One who goes with you. He will not leave you nor forsake you."

During my roughest times, a few songs ministered to me, reminding me that God held my heart in the palm of his hands:

- "The Anchor Holds" by Ray Boltz—God is our anchor, and he holds us during the storms of life. Just imagine, when you are going through the rough waters of life, that you are the boat and God is the anchor. He holds you in place. You can't go anywhere even when you feel rocked by the waves. You will feel the waves pushing and pulling, but you are secure because your anchor is holding you.
- "I Have to Believe" by Rita Springer—The words to this song are beyond perfect when you are going through the storms of life. God can move your mountains, and He is faithful to do that for you. We need to believe and ask God to help us with our unbelief.
- "It's Gonna Be Worth It" by Rita Springer—This song ministered to me, helping me trust that everything I was going through

was going to be worth the heartache, the loneliness, and the uncertainty.
- "Take me to the King" by Tamela Mann—Wow! When you are down and out. This song is a song of surrender. Only God can take a broken heart and turn it into something of beauty.

He wants you to know He is holding your heart right now. He's always right there with you and just wants you to trust Him with your heart.

Remember to turn to Him

Yes, God is always there, but we need to turn to Him and seek Him out. Where are you running to when you are struggling? Do you run to your best friend? Do you run to God? Let me tell you, jumping into Jesus's lap is the best place to run.

My friend Shannon told me, about eight years ago, how when she feels far from God, she puts on worship, and it draws her closer to the Lord. That stuck in my memory bank, and I pull it out when I start to feel some sort of distance between the Lord and me. We can so easily get caught up in our day-to-day and just go through the motions. When that happens, we tend to feel dry. We need the Holy Spirit to pour into our lives. To fill us back up. We can't pour into others' lives if we are empty. Our Heavenly Father is waiting so patiently for us to say, "Fill me up, Lord."

I can't imagine how people go through life without the Lord. Sister friend, please trust God with your heart. Run to him and get filled up. Let Him renew your strength and fall in love with His presence. Go to your room, put on worship, and let the Holy Spirit minister to you. I promise you, it will be worth it!

Has the Lord ever just wrecked you in worship? When God wrecks your heart in worship, it is healing, cleansing, and beautiful. I don't even have the right words to describe it. But you know without a doubt that you were in the presence of the Holy Spirit, and He is just pouring into you and renewing your strength and making you new. Don't let this scare you. It is the closest we can get to God here on Earth. I wish for every one of you to know the true presence of the Lord.

Today I just sat with worship music on for about an hour and a half. If you ever want to give your mind that place of quiet and peace, just put on worship. The calm that comes over you, you can't put a price tag on. Some or a lot of you might already do this. God wants that one-on-one time with you aside from your daily devotions, just time to reconnect with Him and let him minister to your spirit. He will put people in your heart to pray for, download new ideas in your mind, and just cleanse you of the everyday things that weigh you down. It's a beautiful time.

A wakeup call from God

Sometimes God allows us to get sick or be in a situation that lays us out. I truly believe He wants our time and attention when He allows this. I call this "God pinning me down." I'm naturally very energetic. I wake up full of energy and ready to go. This drives some people nuts. My energy can be too much for someone who is mellow and takes their time waking up. I wake up and start cleaning, doing laundry, and making breakfast all by 7:00 a.m. Then I pop my anxious little head into the kids' room to tell them breakfast is ready. Later I found out they didn't want to be woken up that early and would rather I had breakfast ready at 9:00 a.m. or later. This threw off my juju.

All this to say, God needs to slow me down from time to time. Slowing me down allows me to stop and say, "Okay, God, what are you trying to tell me? What is on your heart? What do you want me to do? Who do you want me to pray for?" He is faithful in answering those questions. So I better be ready to start writing. He downloads fast with me. If I don't write things down, I will forget something or most things. That's part of my very energetic mindset. Sometimes I feel like Dory from *Finding Nemo*. But seriously, God wants our attention. He will do whatever it takes to get it when He wants it.

Has God ever asked you to do something and you feel like you wouldn't know where to start? That is what God did with me with this book. I thought, "Why would anyone want to know my story? How would it even apply to someone else?" I have to believe that this is for at least one person who is reading it. Because God pinned me down many times to work on it.

It's funny how we aren't always aware of His presence in our lives. But when He is chasing after you and asking you to do something for Him, He is there. He hasn't nor will He ever leave you.

Learning how God speaks to you

When you have a relationship with God, you learn how He speaks to you. With me, He is bold and just says it like it is. I think that is because I can be like Dory. It has to be a direct order. Straight forward. No beating around the bush. I have a lot of nieces, and they have come to me over the years to pray with them from time to time. One time I was praying over one of my nieces and the Lord kept repeating Himself. I was shook. God doesn't do that when He speaks to me. So I had to ask her, "Does God repeat Himself when He is speaking to you?" "She said yes, that's how I know it's from God." Okay, that makes sense. It doesn't matter how God speaks to her versus how He speaks to me. But it was amazing to witness that He will speak to people in the way that works best for them. I thought that was pretty cool.

How do you recognize God's voice?

This is important because this is another example of God's love for us. He is gentle and personal with each and every one of us. My grandma says she doesn't hear him like this. She said she will have a feeling in her spirit. So, please don't compare how you hear from the Lord with how your best friend hears from the Lord.

We all have a very unique relationship with God, which makes what we have with Him so special.

Regardless of the how, know that God is there for you always! We sometimes just need to tune in.

God will use any means to show you that He is there with you. He can use the people in your life. I was blessed with the best tribe a girl could ask for. None of them were shy when it came to telling me when I was out of line. They knew they could be honest with me. My cousin Teresa asked me one night if I was mad at God. This was after I had first separated from my ex-husband. I instantly said, "No." Well, God used her words. They weighed on me until I came to grips with the fact that I was mad at God. I had no right to be mad at God, but I was mad at Him. The enemy is so sly that he had worked me in a way I didn't realize until Teresa brought it to my attention.

Just because it doesn't feel good doesn't mean it isn't from God. God showed me that He saw my heart by using Teresa's voice. That is how much He loves me. He isn't going to allow me to be or stay mad at Him. That would have gone nowhere good. God wanted that nipped in the bud and dealt with immediately. I am so thankful for Teresa's obedience to speak up. I needed the tough love.

Please take some time and ask the Lord how He has shown up for you. You might not have realized it at the time. It might have felt uncomfortable at the moment. But it was truthful and God is truth. Journal below what the Lord shows you.

Journal Notes

Journal Notes

Chapter 11

Grace

Everyone has an opinion or a belief on what is a sin and what should be condemned. But people do not know you and your life experiences that caused certain choices. But God does, and God will extend grace.

My story

When I was only fifteen, my boyfriend of a year and a half took my virginity, even though I had said no.

I was heartbroken and walked around with a cloud of grief following me everywhere for a good while. But out of blind love, I forgave him and decided if we were going to be sexually active, I needed to get on birth control.

Little did I know that the first thing the doctor would do is take a pregnancy test. It was silly, as I had only had sex once. But turns out I was over a month pregnant and was due on my sixteenth birthday. I decided not to tell my mom, only my friend's mom, who suggested I write down the pros and cons. Heck... What were the pros and cons?

Meanwhile, my boyfriend was gathering money from his friends to pay for an abortion.

When I told him I wasn't sure that was what I wanted, the boy I loved so much turned on me and said, "If you have this baby, I will kill you and the baby." He had put his hands on me before, so of course, I believed him 110 percent.

In July of 1984, my aunt, two cousins, my boyfriend, and I took a long drive to an abortion clinic away from the area. This day will be forever embedded in my memory. Before the procedure, a counselor called me in for a meeting. The counselor wasn't much of a counselor. She didn't even explain how I would feel emotionally and physically, nor did she offer another solution. It was a very cold and calloused conversation.

When my name was called, I got up and walked with the nurse down a long corridor. The nurse me, "You are eleven-and-a-half-weeks pregnant now. If you had waited one more day, you wouldn't be able to do this." She didn't tell me how big a baby is at this age, or what has developed. Just that I wouldn't have been allowed to do this tomorrow. It didn't click until it was too late. Those large steel doors slammed shut so loudly! A sound that has stayed with me forever. The nurse was so hard and cold. I guess they harden up after doing this as their job. There were no emotions and definitely no convictions that were noticeable.

My Mess, His Grace!

I woke up in a different room with a pounding headache and the nurse telling me I needed to get up. The nurse gave me Tylenol, some juice, and some cookies and told me to get dressed. I was bleeding badly and still under anesthesia. Not very alert, I did what they said.

My aunt knew it wasn't a good idea to take me straight home, so she went took me to a different aunt's house so I could rest. I was cramping and bleeding so badly that I threw up and couldn't hold down any food. I threw up so much that I was vomiting green bile. I didn't feel sorry for myself, but I knew in her heart that this just wasn't right. Nothing about this entire situation was okay.

I couldn't talk about it and couldn't wrap my mind around what I had just done, so I decided it was time to start drinking and partying more than ever. I couldn't escape how I felt, though I tried to get lost in it all.

Right when I was really losing myself, I decided to move in with my aunt and uncle right before my sixteenth birthday, which I had no desire to celebrate. How could I? I was living in what felt like a foreign town with my mind trying to sort through my roller-coaster life. I wanted so badly to take that day in July back and not go through with it. I wanted to celebrate the birth of my baby and the life that I had stolen from him/her.

While living with my aunt and uncle, I got involved in church and went to a youth retreat. One night by the campfire, one girl brought up the subject of abortion and shared her strong and passionate opinion of how wrong it is and how she can't stand girls that do that. I stayed quiet. The leader noticed and chimed in and asked me, "Have you had an abortion?" I broke down in tears and talked about how much I regretted it. The leader was so warm and loving and showed me that God had forgiven me. She suggested that I name the baby, so I could give it to God. I named the baby Rikky.

This was a night of healing and restoration for me. I still remember every July what I did, and every February, I think of how old the baby would have been. I have dreams of a little girl with long brown curly hair. And although I am sad, I remember I gave Rikky to God and know one day I will get to meet Rikky face to face and love her.

Giving grace

So many people have opinions on abortion, and while I personally think abortion is not a good choice, I do not know the hearts and situations of those who make that decision. Because I have been there, I can have grace. But I need to remember to have grace for all situations and choices people have made.

We all have sinned and fallen short of God's glory. If I could undo what I did thirty-eight years ago, I would in a heartbeat.

Even after giving Rikky to the Lord all those years ago, I still think about her all the time. I ask Jesus to tell her I love her and give her hugs from me. The deep root that took hold in my life and carried over into other areas of my life from this horrible choice has peeked its ugly head more often than I would like.

God's grace never ceases to amaze me. I saw the baby's dad about a year and a half later, and we went for a walk down by the beach in the evening. He gave me a genuine apology, and I really saw how I needed to give him the same grace that God had given to me. I didn't mention how I named the baby, not really sure why other than that it was between God and myself and the girls that were sitting around the campfire that night at the retreat.

About a year ago, I heard from the baby's dad. He had been in prison for the past twenty years, and he found me on Facebook. I didn't know that he had struggled with the abortion like I did. I thought this whole time that he was perfectly fine with it. When we chatted, he said, "What we did was horrible, and I'm so sorry. I wasn't healthy back then and had no right to be in a relationship." He was very genuinely apologetic. He had come to know the Lord, and for whatever reason, God wanted to extend more grace to him. This is when I felt prompted to share the night at the campfire, the dreams, and how I named the baby Rikky. He was so happy that I named the baby and very thankful I shared it with him.

God's grace is for everyone who wants it. He doesn't have a list of who He won't extend grace to. Please know I'm not sharing this story with you because I am proud of it by any means. I just want you to know that God's grace is there for you. You just need to receive it. Your sin may be different than mine or may have happened because of different circumstances, but it doesn't matter. God died for *all* sin.

This is why when people don't believe in God, I can't wrap my head around it. I have seen God's grace in action. I know God is real, and I know His forgiveness and grace are real. Please don't allow the enemy to hold you in the bondage of unforgiveness toward yourself. This kind of bondage is a very dark pit. Please ask God to show where you need to forgive and extend grace to yourself. Journal below and ask God to help you forgive yourself. Ask Him to show you where He has given you grace. And ask Him to show you where you need to extend grace to others. He has a future for you, sister friend.

Journal Notes

Journal Notes

Conclusion

The choices you make in your life will determine your path. They can lead you to a life of peace or indifference. But if we make choices that are good for us, we will reap the benefits of joy. Just remember to pick yourself up if you fall. There is always a way out, and God has hope for each and every one of us.

Thank You!!

Thank You So Much For Reading My Book!

I would really appreciate all your input concerning how the book spoke to you. This will help me make my future books better.

Please take a couple of minutes now to leave a helpful review on Amazon, letting me know what you think of this book.

Thank you so much!

—Kristie McPheeters

Made in the USA
Coppell, TX
07 March 2023